CLAIRE BRETECHER

Frustration

TRANSLATED FROM THE FRENCH
BY ANGELA MASON AND PAT FOGARTY

METHUEN · LONDON

First published in Great Britain in 1982 by Claire Bretecher and distributed by Methuen London Ltd, 11 New Fetter Lane, London EC4P 4EE.

Reprinted in 1985
ISBN: 0-413-51250-9

MAGGIE AND MEN

THE FIANCÉ

mood music

NO MORE FOR ANTHEA

ALONE IN THE DARK

NOSTALGIA

15

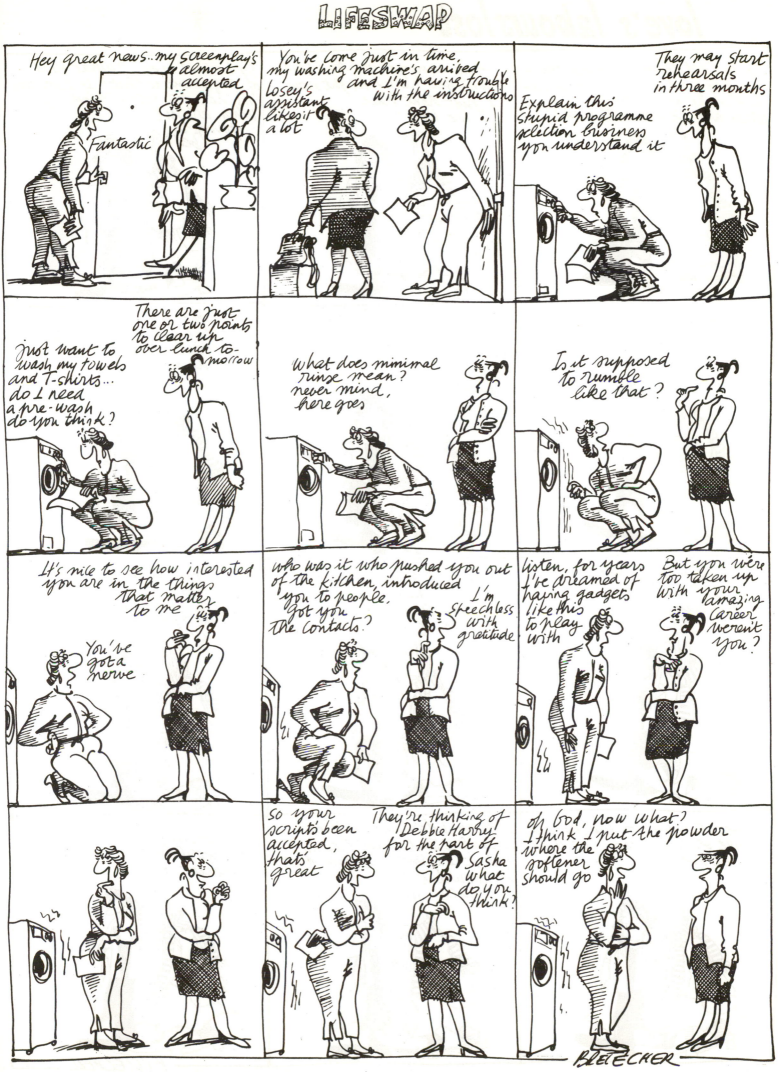

love's labours lost

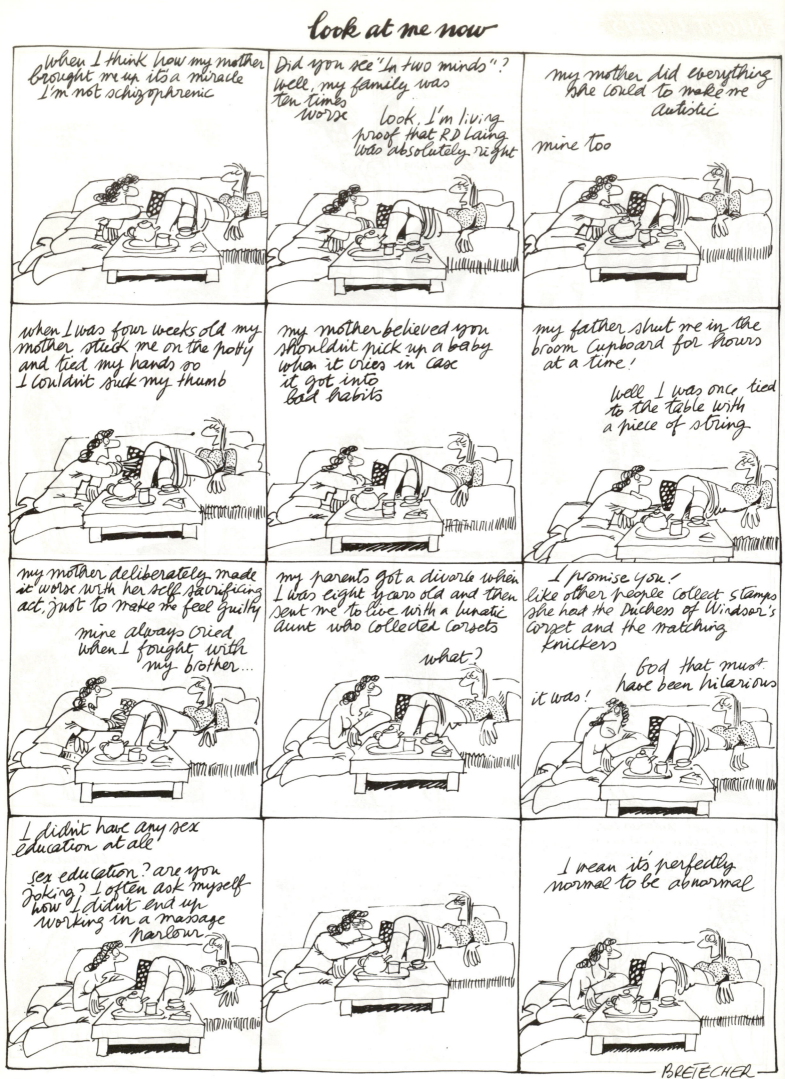

A woman's work

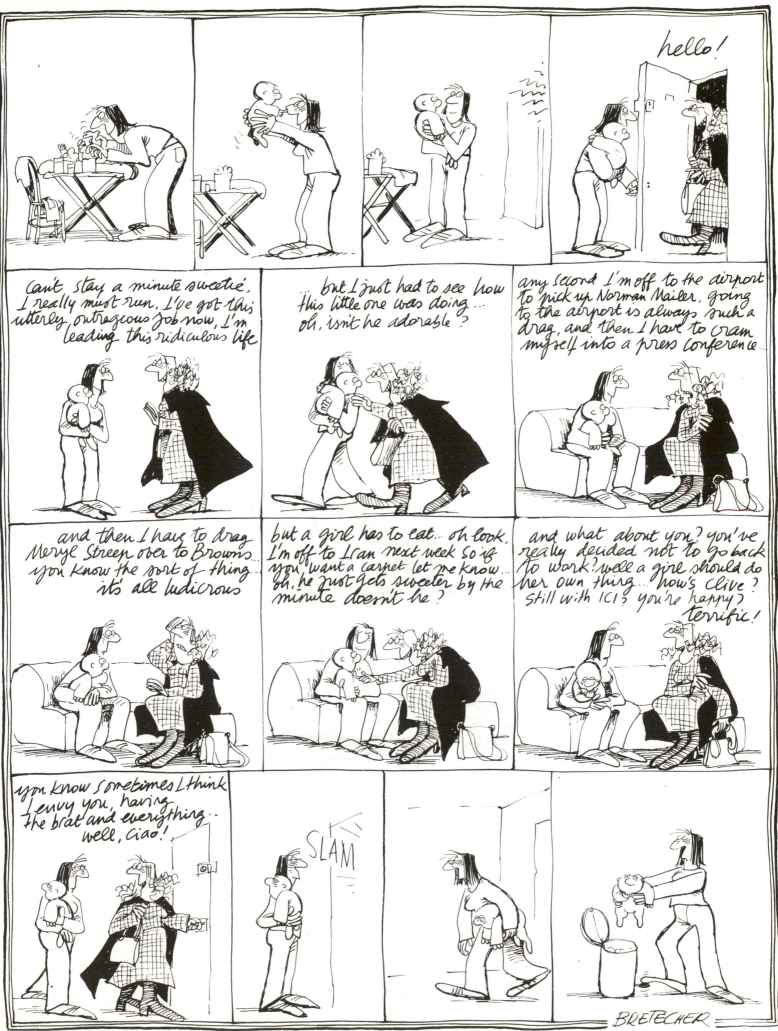

RELIGIOUS HISTORY

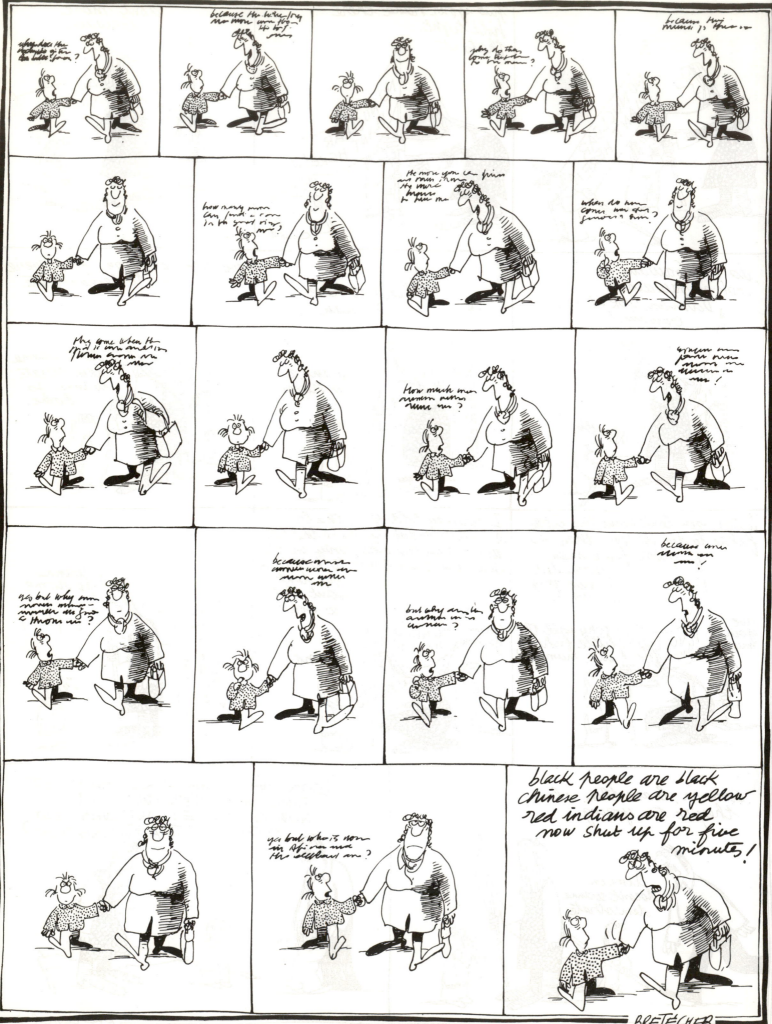

FATHER IMAGE

JEALOUSY

SUICIDE

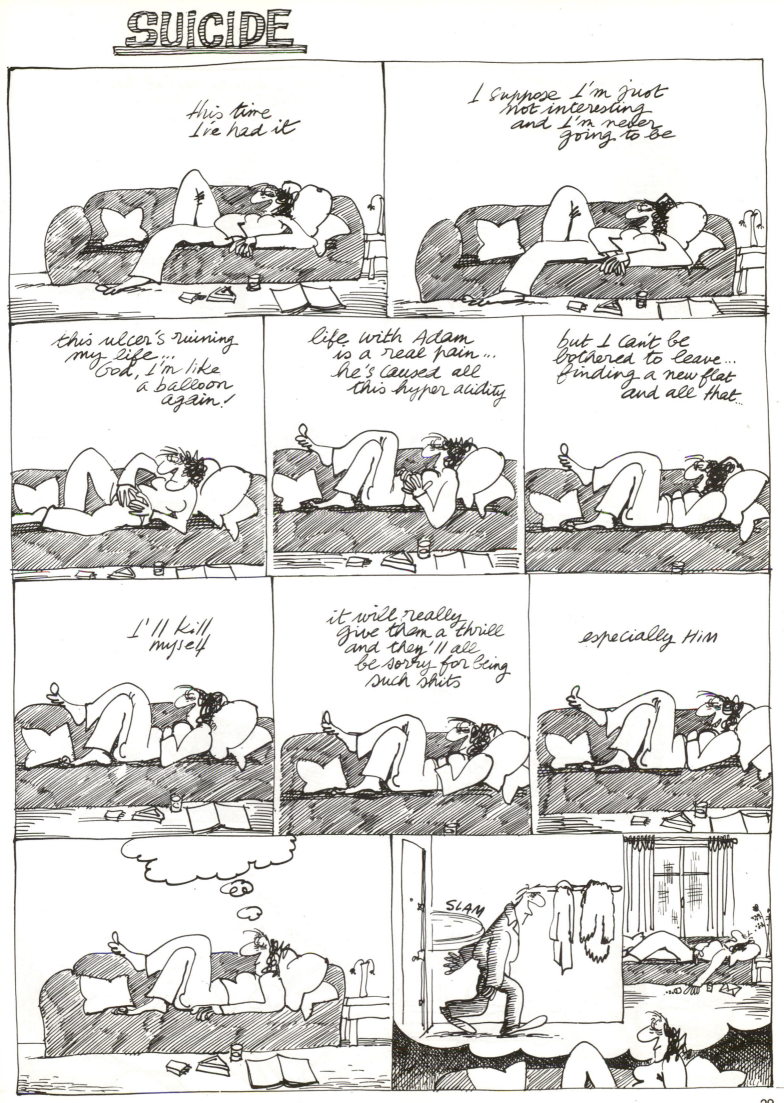

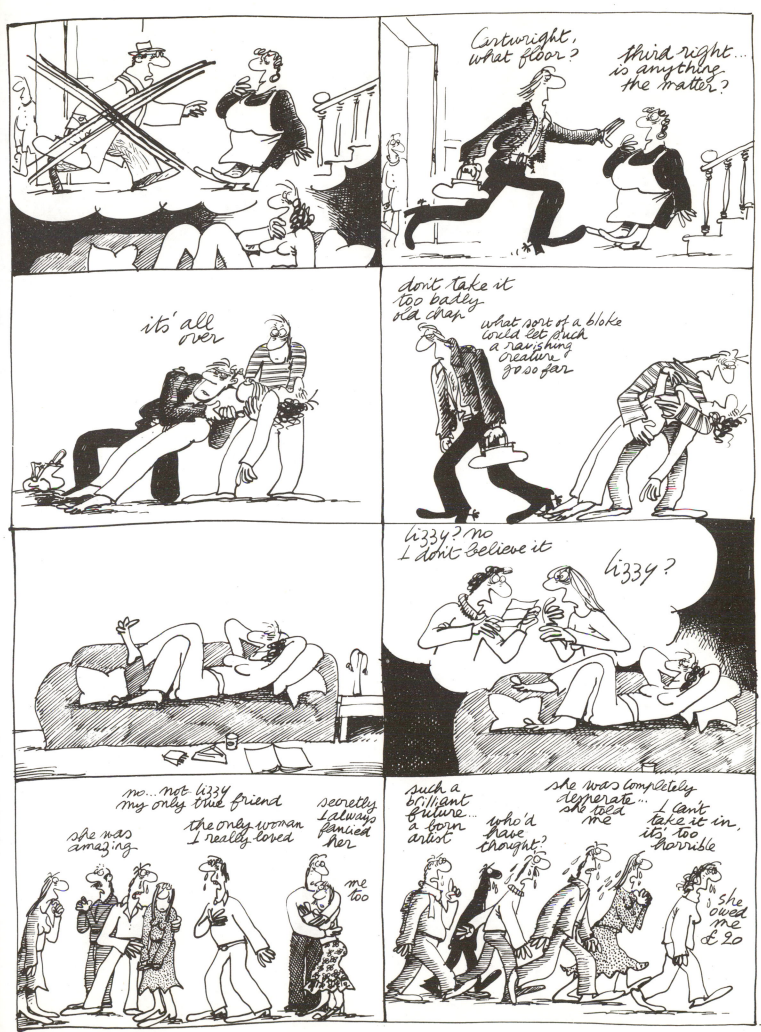

point blank

Corinne

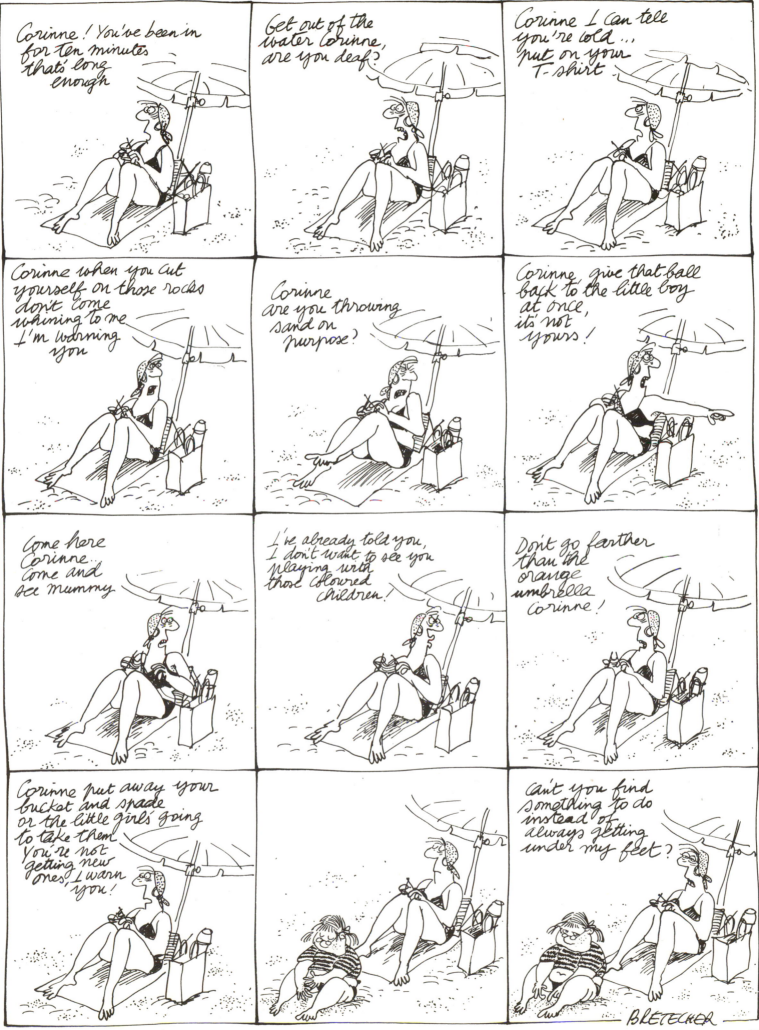

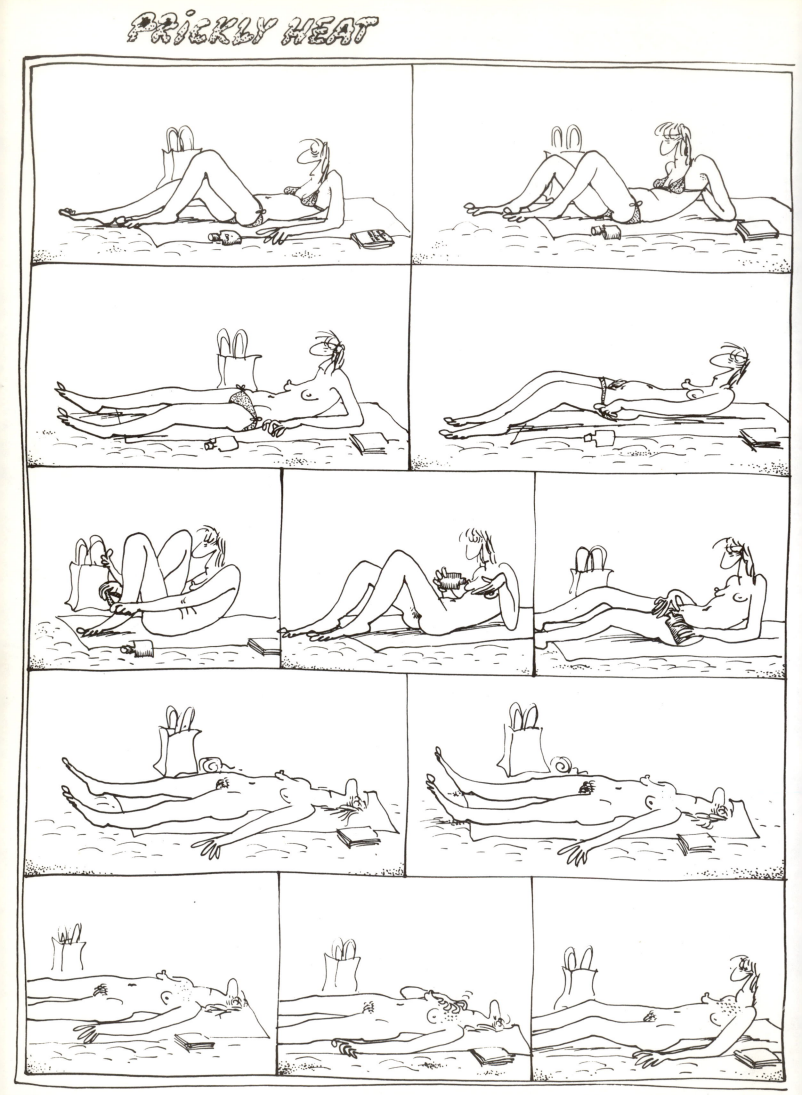

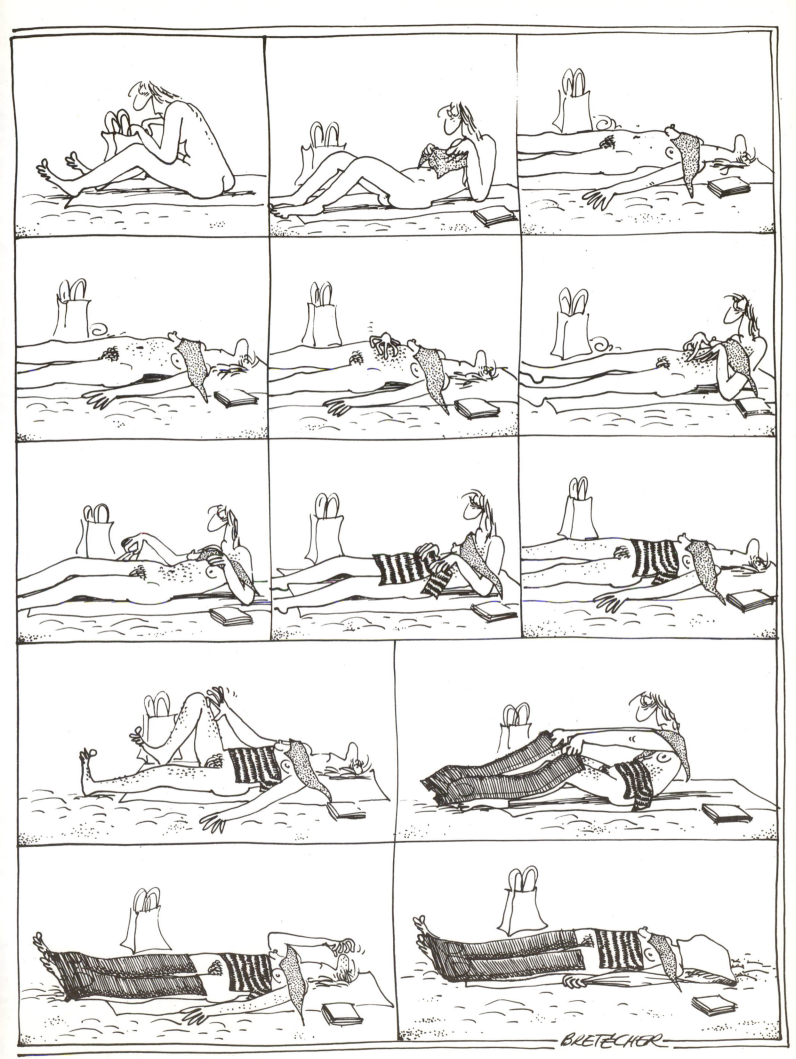

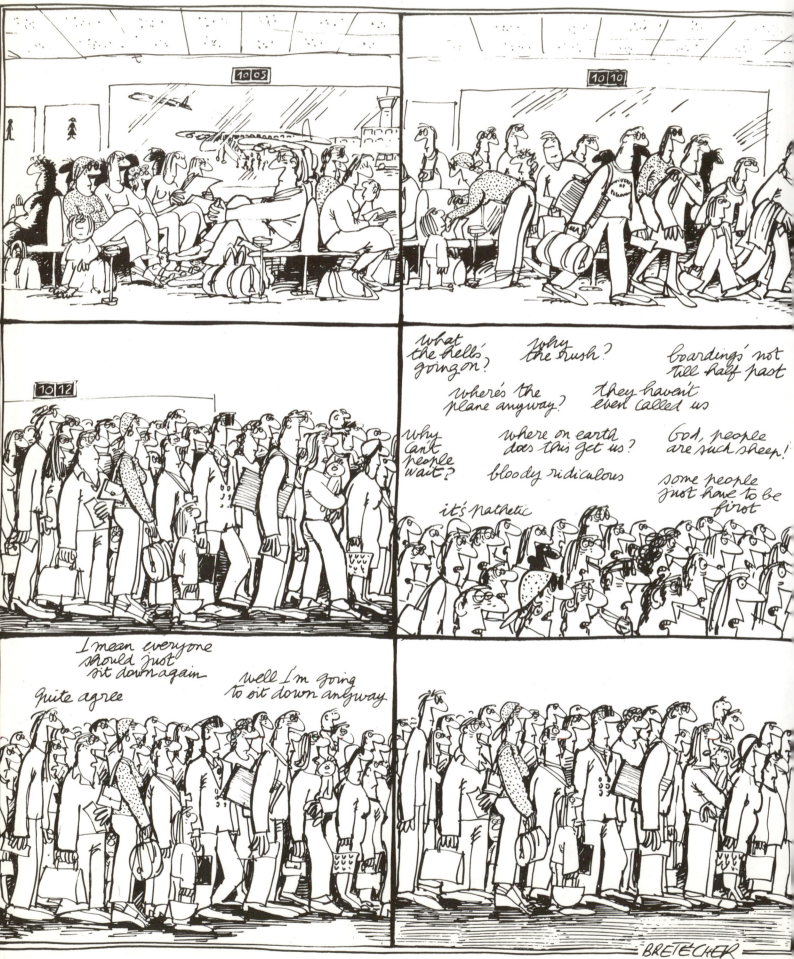

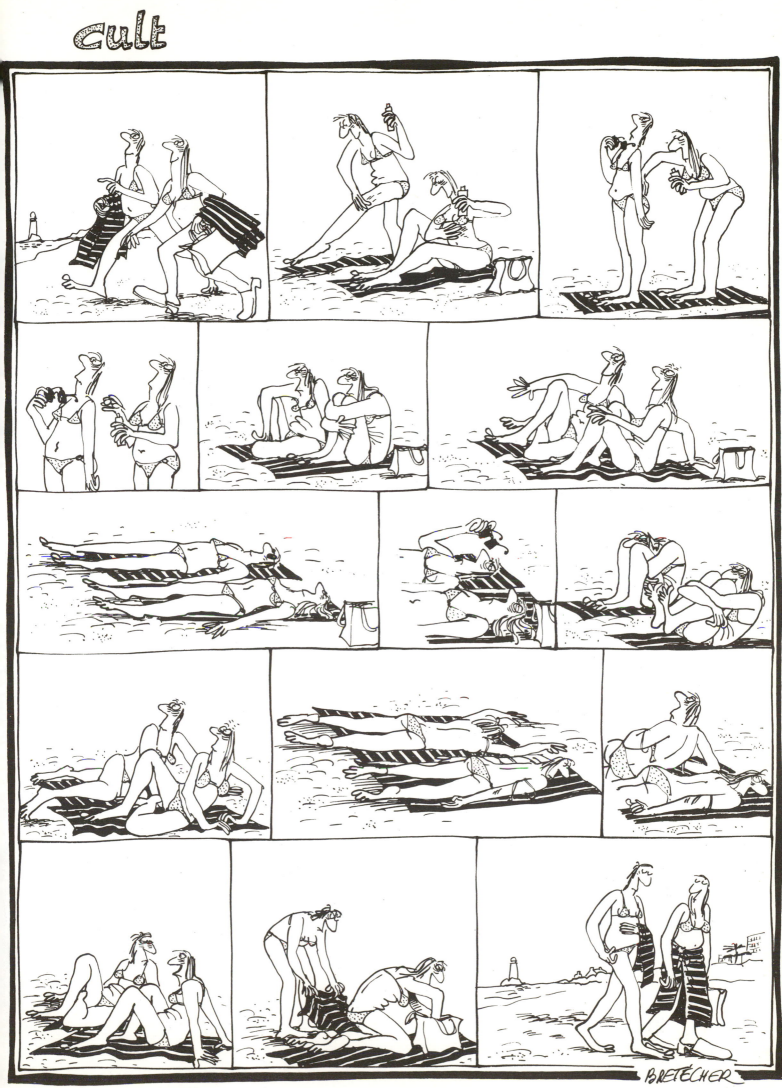

BRETECHER

EUGEEENE !

SMALL ADS.

The Pits

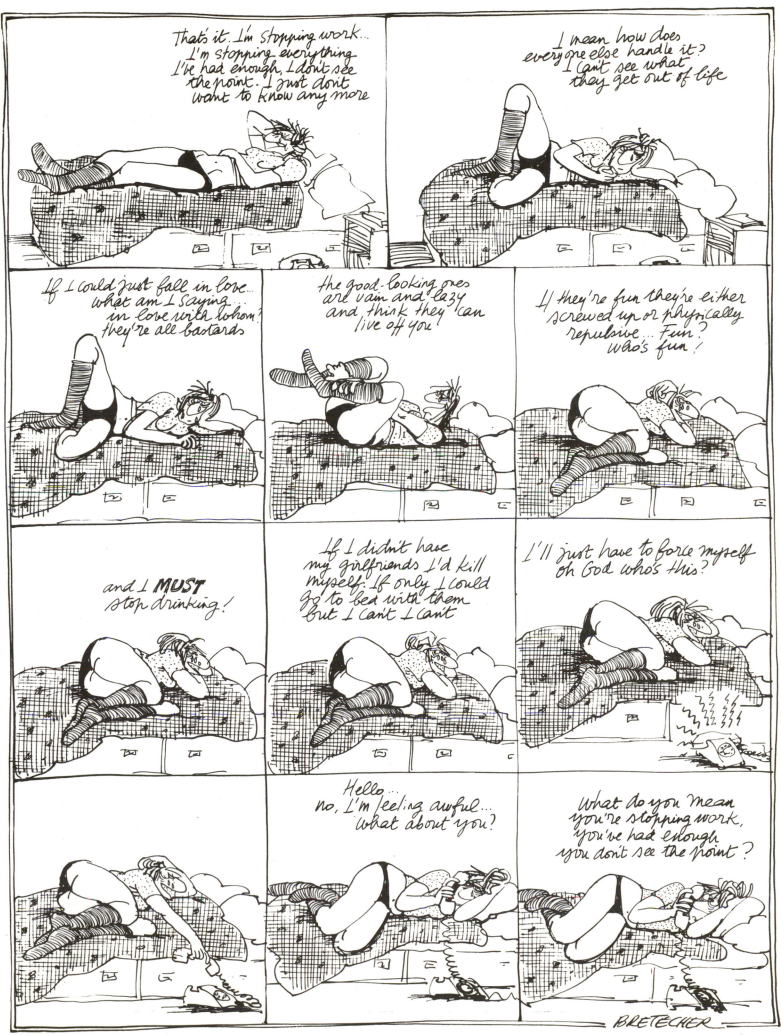

CREATiON

THUNDER THIGHS

SHORT- SIGHTED

body beautiful

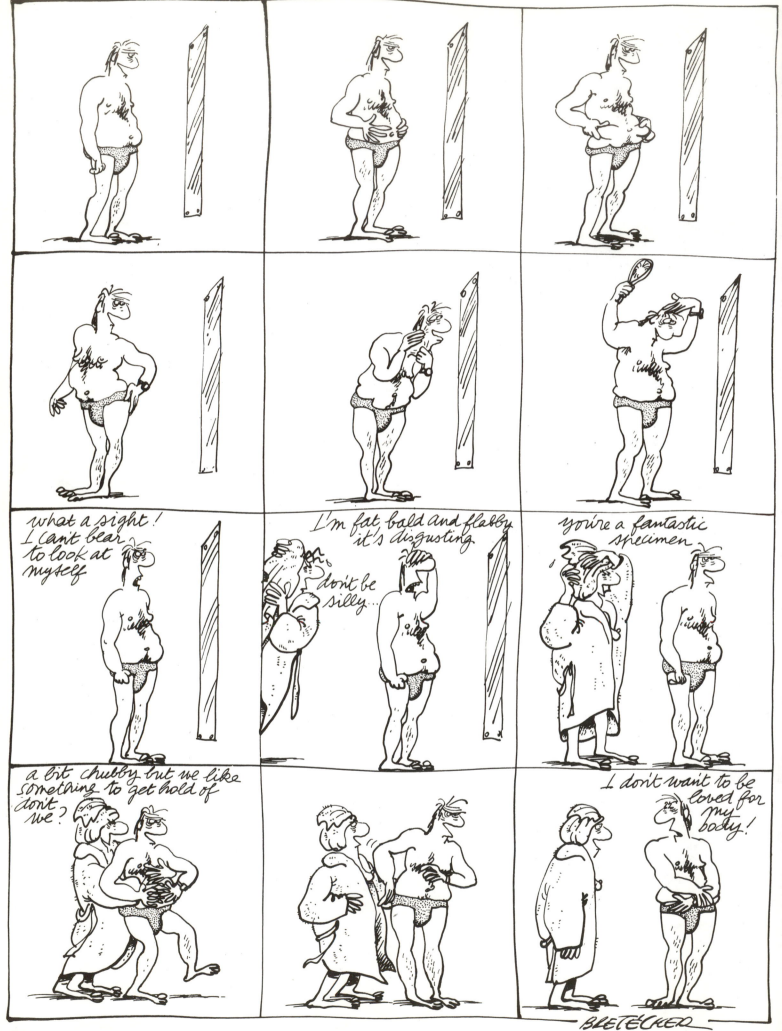

...and that was Wayne Fonteyn in an extract from 'DOGS DAYS' choreographed by Kenneth Ashton at the Camden Dance Floor

untie July 14

BRETECHER

WRITINGS

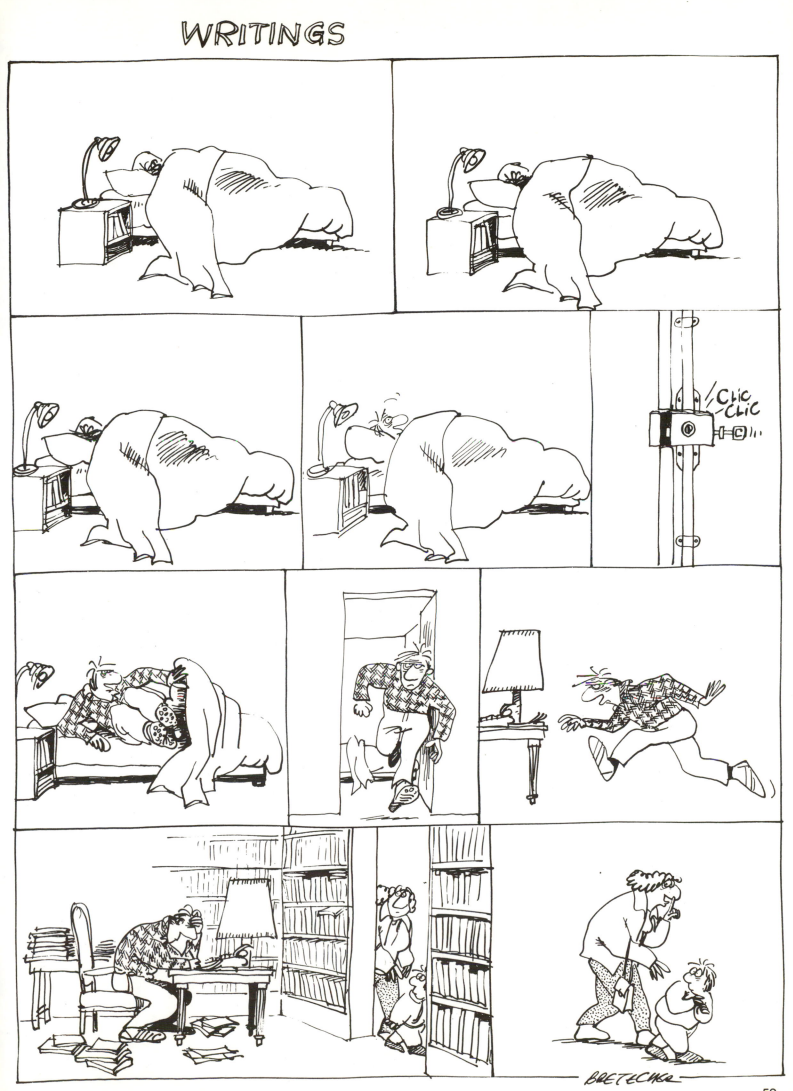

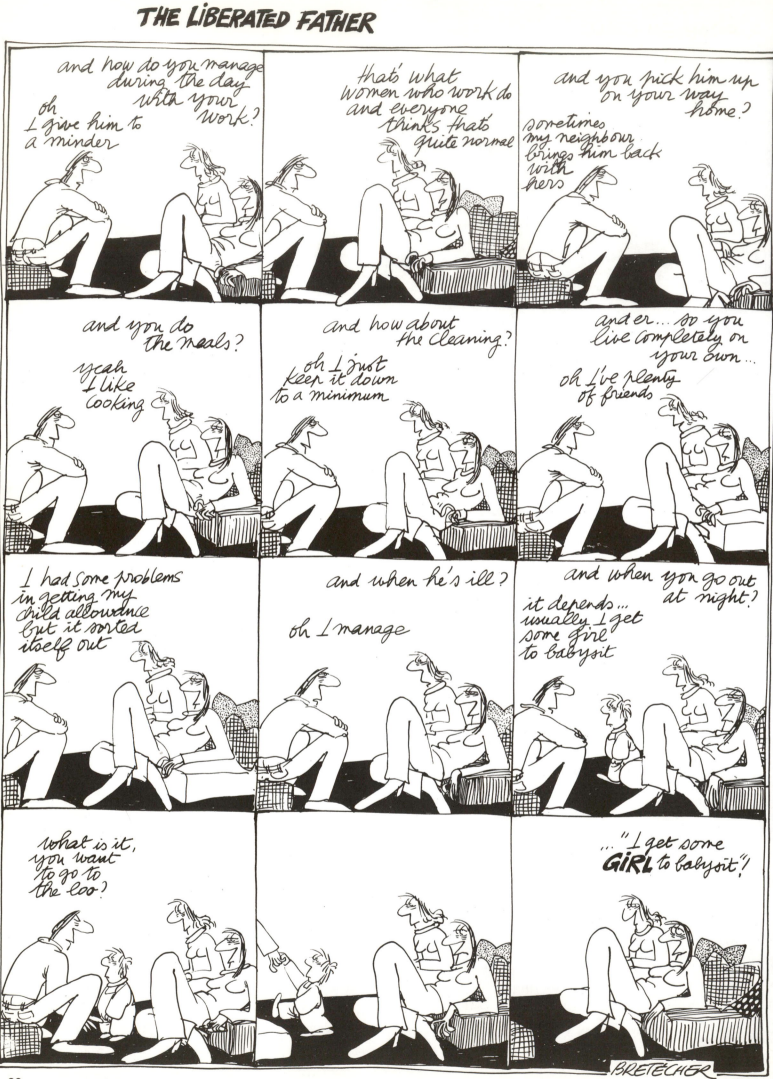

A PROBLEM CHILD

a fairy tale

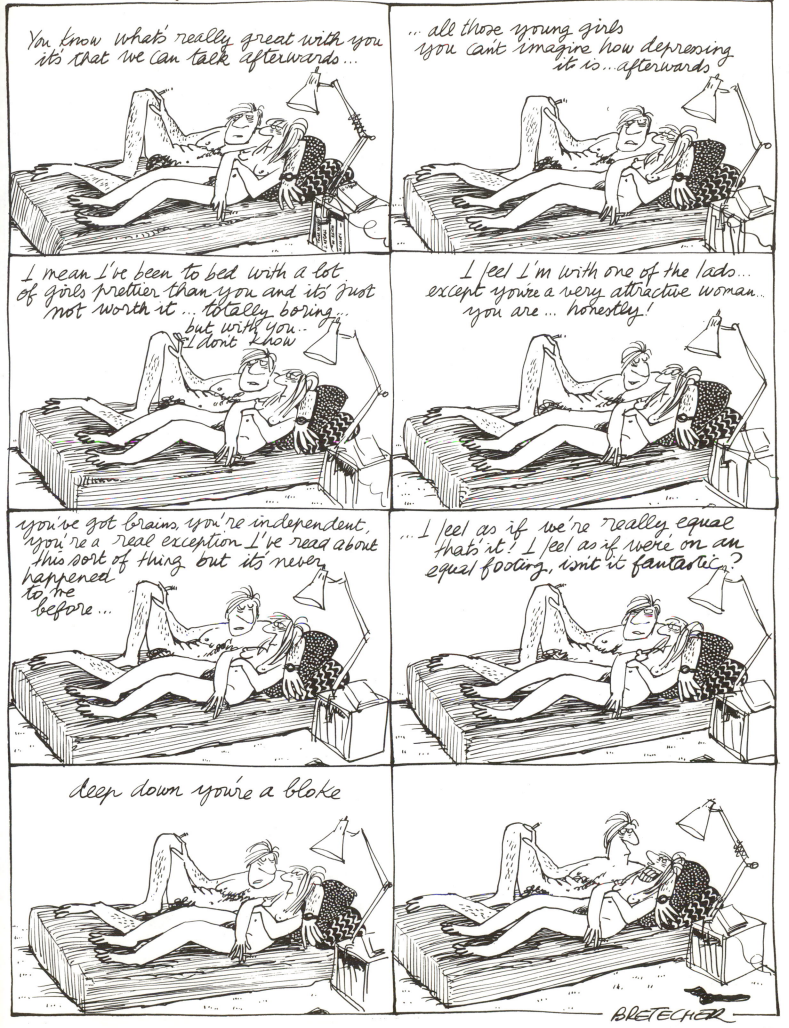

A TIGHT SPOT

In fact medical opinion stresses that the testicles should be kept unconstricted and at a temperature slightly lower than the rest of the body. Squashed and overheated in too tight trousers they start to lose their magical powers. In fact Professor Laing recently announced that British men are making love less and less and their sperm is alarmingly impoverished.

BRETECHER

SOME DAY MY PRINCE WILL COME

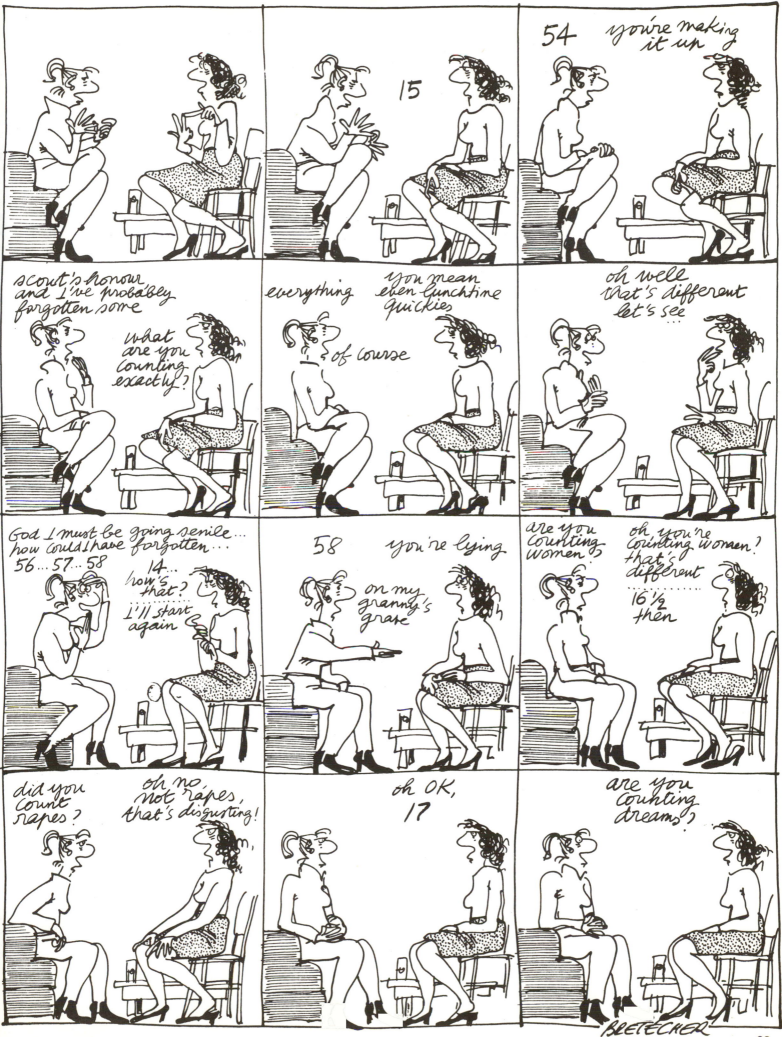

PRINTED BY
PRINTER INDUSTRIA GRAFICA SA   PROVENZA, 388   BARCELONA
SANT VICENÇ DELS HORTS   1982
D.L.B. 24361-1982